Mary, Queen of Scots

AND ALL THAT

Allan Burnett

Illustrated by Scoular Anderson

First published in 2006 by
Birlinn Limited
West Newington House
10 Newington Road
Edinburgh
EH9 1QS

Reprinted in 2016 by BC Books
an imprint of Birlinn Ltd

www.bcbooksforkids.co.uk

ISBN: 978 1 78027 388 4

British Library Cataloguing-in-Publication Data
A catalogue record for this book is available from the British Library

Designed by James Hutcheson
Typeset by Iolaire Typesetting, Newtonmore
Printed and bound by Grafica Veneta, Italy
www.graficaveneta.com

For my niece
Orla

Contents

Prologue

Terror struck Mary, Queen of Scots, as a gang rushed forward and plunged their daggers into the man cowering behind her. His name was David Rizzio, one of Mary's most loyal friends. And as her trusty servant slumped to the ground, lifeless, Mary wondered whether she would be next.

To find out whether the queen survived this scene of slaughter, you must read on. But be warned – Mary's life is packed with grisly murders, strange mysteries, weird and wonderful costumes, passionate romances and death-defying dramas. It twists and turns like a poisonous snake – and will keep you guessing up to the very end.

But first, we must begin at the beginning. So settle back in your favourite cosy spot, imagine your glass of juice or mug of tea is a sixteenth-century goblet filled with fine French wine and picture yourself standing in the grounds of a magnificent palace, as snowflakes begin falling all around . . .

1

The ice queen

A thick blanket of snow was settling over Linlithgow Palace on Friday, 8 December 1542, when the cries of a newborn baby girl were suddenly heard inside. The baby's name was Mary, the future Queen of Scots.

The windows of the royal bedchamber had glass panes, which sheltered Mary and her French mum, Mary of Guise, from the frost outside. Glass windows were expensive in those days, but Mary's dad, Scotland's King James V, could afford them.

The kingdom of Scotland was rich and Linlithgow was one of the finest royal houses in Europe. The palace's stone walls and woodwork were beautifully carved. Covering the walls were fine tapestries and cloths made of gold thread.

Each room was warmed by blazing fires, which cast light up onto the finely painted ceilings. What had once upon a time been a cold and draughty castle was now a luxurious place to live. In other words, primitive mediaeval styles were out, and a fancy new fashion called the Renaissance was in.

But the palace wasn't the only thing changing. The whole kingdom was changing too, and in ways that made a lot of people worried.

A group of men called Reformers were going around Scottish towns and villages trying to persuade folk to join a new religion called the Protestant Church. This was worrying because changing your religion wasn't like changing your socks or wearing your hair differently – it was a deadly serious business.

Up until then, everyone in Scotland, like everybody else in Europe, had been part of the same religion – the Catholic Church. In other words, everybody was singing from the same hymn sheet.

But the Reformers claimed the Catholic Church was corrupt, which meant it was run by greedy and lazy good-for-nothings, who took money and land from the Scottish people but didn't put it to good use. The Reformers also argued that the Catholic Church kept the people in the dark about a lot of important matters.

Although lots of Scots began to support the Reformers,

and began turning against the Catholic Church, the Reformers had a problem. Mary and her family, the royals, were still Catholics – and they ruled the kingdom.

Mary's dad liked the Catholic Church because he was allowed to take its money to pay for expensive things, like Linlithgow Palace. He also liked the fact that the Church kept people in the dark about important matters, which he reckoned were best left up to him. The king worried that if the Catholic Church was done away with, people might start thinking about getting rid of other expensive things – like him!

So Mary's dad didn't like the Reformers one bit. In fact, one of James V's favourite pastimes was roasting Reformers at the stake. Large crowds gathered to watch these poor souls being burned or tortured and many people felt sorry for them. Anger at the royals began to grow.

The king thought if he kept burning Reformers or locking them up the problem would go away. He was wrong. Instead, the Protestant Church just got bigger.

All of this was storing up future troubles for little Mary as she slept in her cradle. But the problem of Scotland's religion wasn't the only dangerous puzzle she would one day have to try to solve. There was also the question of how to deal with some very quarrelsome neighbours.

2

Baptism of fire

Just six days after Mary was born, her dad died of a mysterious illness. It was announced that Mary would soon become queen of Scots, even though she was still just a baby.

As soon as Mary was strong enough to be taken outside, she was baptised a Catholic. Her French mum, Mary of Guise, was also a fan of the old Church. And why not? The Catholic religion still had its good sides, too. Many people preferred it to Protestantism and wanted to stick with it.

Besides her mum, baby Mary had lots of people wanting to decide things for her. A group of powerful men, the Scottish nobles, formed a Council of Regency to rule Scotland until Mary was old enough to do it herself. Mary's mum was now the Queen regnant, which meant she was also very powerful, and spent a lot of her time arguing with the council about what was best for Mary and the kingdom.

Another reason why people wanted to decide things for Mary was because she was a girl. It seems silly, but people then tended to think a queen wasn't strong or wise enough to rule on her own. This meant a lot of people, especially men, interfered in Mary's private business throughout her whole life.

Whether people liked it or not, Mary was the rightful heir to the Scottish throne. Her mum and dad had had two boys before her, but they had both died very young.

James V had also had lots of other children, but their mothers were not his good lady wife! These half-siblings of Mary were therefore considered illegitimate, which meant they had only a weak claim to Mary's crown. But a few of them still had their eyes on it all the same.

And they weren't the only ones. The English and French royal families were interested in controlling Scotland, too.

England and France were almost always quarrelling with each other. Because Scotland was so close to both kingdoms, it was stuck in the middle – a bit like being caught between two boxers in a ring:

In the red corner: the English. If they could control Scotland, the French would not be able to use Scotland as a spot to attack England from behind.

In the blue corner: the French, who wanted Scotland on their side so the English would never know which direction the next punch was coming from.

To keep Scotland on their side, the English wanted to marry Mary off to one of their princes, so he could become king of Scots. Meanwhile, the French plan was to marry Mary off to one of *their* princes.

The trouble for the French was that the English had a real heavyweight in their corner who hated to lose at anything. His name was Henry VIII . . .

Cradle–snatchers

The fight over Mary began when the grumpy and big-bellied Henry VIII unlocked the Tower of London and released some Scottish prisoners. In return for their freedom, Henry VIII made the prisoners agree to become his secret agents.

The agents were ordered to snatch Mary and take her to England, where she would be married to Henry VIII's five-year-old son and heir, Prince Edward. Then, until Mary and Edward became grown-ups, Henry VIII would rule Scotland by himself.

It was a cunning plan indeed, but Henry VIII realised Mary was more than just a pawn in England's battle with France.

When word spread of what Henry VIII was up to, many Scots were not amused. They had no intention of letting the English control their queen, or their kingdom.

Henry VIII's Scottish agents and stooges tried to arrange a marriage between little Mary and Edward with an agreement called the Treaty of Greenwich in July 1543. But Mary's mum (who was French, remember) and the rest of the Scots simply tore it up.

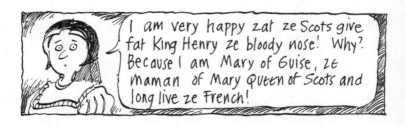

I am very happy zat ze Scots give fat King Henry ze bloody nose! Why? Because I am Mary of Guise, ze maman of Mary Queen of Scots and long live ze French!

The French were most likely to win the contest for Mary and Scotland. The fact that James V had taken Mary of Guise as his wife proved many Scots preferred being closer to the French than the English.

The Scots liked the fact that the French wanted to be allies and friends instead of trying to conquer Scotland. The English, on the other hand, were *always* trying to conquer Scotland!

It suited the French and the Scots to unite against their common enemy, England. In fact, the Scots and the French had been helping each other out against the English for centuries. This special friendship was called the Auld Alliance.

But despite the fact many Scots preferred the French, Mary of Guise was too crafty to believe Henry VIII would take the hint and go away. She knew the English king would stop at nothing to get his hands on her daughter.

So before Henry VIII's agents got a chance to snatch baby Mary, she was moved from Linlithgow to Stirling Castle, a mighty stone fortress on a steep rock. She would be safe there, at least for a while . . .

Rough wooing

When Henry VIII realised Mary was being hidden from him, he didn't take too kindly to it. In fact, he was red-faced with rage.

While Henry's temper began boiling over, little Mary was officially crowned queen of Scots at Stirling Castle in September 1543. Well, actually, since she was still only nine months old, the crown was far too big for her – so it had to be held over her head.

But Mary was still given the sacred powers of majesty, which made her an anointed queen. In other words, very special indeed!

Without further ado, the Scots also made a deal with the French to make the Auld Alliance stronger. This was another signal to Henry VIII that the Scots would sooner eat raw haggis than marry their baby queen to the English Prince Edward. So how did Henry react? Did he:

Well, considering Henry VIII was a king who liked chopping the heads off his own wives, it's no surprise that he went for option C. Determined to kidnap Mary and bring her back to England, Henry VIII burned and pillaged southern Scotland. He planned to continue until the Scots stopped playing hard to get and handed over their queen. This bloody episode is known as Henry's 'rough wooing' of Mary.

But Henry VIII caved in before the Scots did – by dying in January 1547.

Since Prince Edward (or King Edward VI as he now was) was still only nine, it was up to his uncle the Duke of Somerset to call the shots. Somerset also thought marrying Mary off to Edward was a good idea, so he sent the English army back into Scotland to try to kidnap the queen.

Things started getting hairy for little Mary. Even mighty

Stirling Castle wasn't safe for her, so she was taken away to a place called the Lake of Menteith and rowed out to a secret island to be hidden. On the island she was looked after in a very serious religious place called Inchmahome Priory – not a fun spot for a four-year-old.

Luckily, Mary's mum had a plan. It was time to send Mary to marry a French prince! Great idea – Mary would be out of English reach, while the French would be obliged to help defend Scotland against more English attacks.

So what was in it for the French, besides gaining a place where they could thump the English from behind? Well, the king of France, who was called Henri, had another reason for liking the idea.

It was agreed Mary would be sent to France to be brought up and married to King Henri's son, the dauphin François. (Dauphin was the French word for a prince who was heir to the French throne.)

This meant Mary would one day also become queen of

France. Remember, Mary was not only queen of Scots, but had a claim to the English throne as well. So it's clear that becoming queen of France too would make this little girl one of the most important people in Europe.

5

Escape

Not everybody in Scotland was happy about Mary going to France. Remember the Protestant Reformers? By now, they included lots of powerful Scottish nobles. These Protestant nobles grumbled about the fact that France was a mostly Catholic country. They wanted Mary to become a Protestant, but there was fat chance of that happening now.

But many other Scots were delighted to see Mary going somewhere safe, and they were relieved her marriage would help protect Scotland against English attack. Above all, they were delighted lots of French claret (fine wine) and other goodies would now pour into Scotland because the two nations were best buddies.

If there was anything really sad about Mary leaving her homeland, it was that she had to leave her mum behind. Mary of Guise had to stay in Scotland to keep an eye on things. So, at the age of only five and a half, Mary waved goodbye to her mum on 29 July 1548 and, a few days later, left in a boat bound for France.

At least Mary didn't have to travel alone. In fact, it was rather crowded on board. The passengers included Mary's guardians and servants, but also some special friends:

THE FOUR MARYS

THESE LITTLE GIRLS ALL SHARED MARY'S FIRST NAME — WHICH MUST HAVE BEEN CONFUSING...

Mary, do you want to try on your new dress?

Yes!

TOGETHER, THEY LOVED SINGING AND DANCING. EVEN THEIR SECOND NAMES RHYMED: MARY FLEMING, MARY BEATON, MARY LIVINGSTON AND MARY SETON.

There wasn't much singing or dancing during the stormy crossing to France. It lasted eighteen days and many of those on board were sick, but not Mary. She was made of strong stuff, which was just as well considering what life had in store for her.

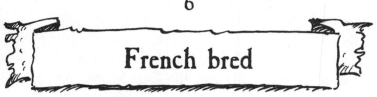

French bred

When Mary got to France, she was introduced to her future husband, the dauphin François, and they were engaged. They made an odd couple. Next to Mary, who was very tall for her age (not to mention pretty), the dauphin was short and puny – although, to be fair, he was a year younger.

But Mary and François did have something in common – they were both smart. Mary was so intelligent she was given the same lessons as the dauphin. It was unusual for a girl to get as good an education as a boy in those days, but it was obvious Mary was a fast learner.

Take languages, for example. Mary already knew how to speak the Scots language of her home country, of course, but she also learned to speak French perfectly.

Life in France wasn't just a pile of dusty schoolbooks, though. François' dad, King Henri, treated Mary as one of his own children. She and the four Marys were given stunning dresses and sparkling jewels to wear, and beautiful palaces and gardens to roam around in.

To top it all, France was warmer and sunnier than cold, damp Scotland. Mary was even treated to a heart-warming long visit from her mum.

During the visit, Mary's mum noticed her daughter was becoming a great dancer who enjoyed music, embroidery and romantic French poetry.

But nobody's perfect. Mary also took ill a lot. She felt pain, vomited and felt very sad. This mysterious illness hounded Mary for the rest of her life.

When Mary's health wasn't suffering, though, she was very sporty. Horse-riding was her favourite pastime.

Besides horses, Mary loved all sorts of animals, including dogs. But she also liked to hunt animals as well. Was the young queen beginning to show a ruthless side?

By the time Mary turned fifteen, people had noticed she was becoming a beautiful young woman. A real stunner. She was much taller than average, with a nice figure and pale skin as smooth as marble. She wore her auburn hair in ringlets.

All Mary needed now was a grand occasion to show off her beauty, like a royal wedding, for example . . .

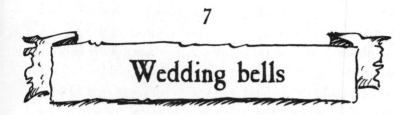

Wedding bells

What could be a more romantic place to tie the knot than the magnificent Notre Dame Cathedral in Paris? Under its huge gothic arches, Mary and François were married on Sunday, 24 April 1558. It was a grand occasion. Mary even gave an impression of the Hunchback of Notre Dame, since she had to stoop slightly to be on the same level as the dauphin at the altar.

But when Mary stood tall, she was stunning in her white wedding dress. It was daring of Mary to choose white. In those days, queens usually only wore white dresses after somebody had just died! But Mary didn't care – she knew she suited white and if other people had a problem with it, then tough.

Was Mary starting to show a headstrong side? Well, at least she had an excuse – she was fifteen, and wanted to show the world that she was becoming a young woman with her own ideas.

Fifteen seems a young age to be married, but in the sixteenth century it was considered old enough. The wedding was followed by a big party in Paris.

There were big celebrations in Scotland, too, with

bonfires and processions. The queen of Scots had taken a big step closer to becoming the queen of France.

In November, Mary also got a step closer to the throne of England. It was a sudden event, but with a bit of a long story behind it . . .

Remember Henry VIII? As you will recall, he died back in 1547, leaving the English throne to Prince Edward (the young suitor for Mary the Scots had rejected). But poor Edward had developed a nasty hacking cough that brought up blood and slime and he only lasted until 1553 before he died of his vile disease, which we now know was tuberculosis.

The English throne had then passed to one of Henry's daughters, Mary Tudor, who was much older but also poorly. Now, in 1558, Mary Tudor died without children, putting our young heroine Mary in the frame to become queen of England.

Young Mary's father-in-law, King Henri, was delighted when poor old Mary Tudor bit the dust. Seeing a chance to make himself more important, Henri began telling everybody that Mary was the rightful heir to the throne of England. He even had a special coat of arms made for her with the coats of arms of France, Scotland, England and Ireland (if you ruled England, you ruled Ireland too) painted in each quarter.

As you can imagine, however, there were people in England who took a different view. As with Scotland and France, England was being torn apart by a great religious quarrel over the kingdom's future.

It was a bit like a tug of war, with the prize being that you got to decide who the next ruler of England would be. On one side were the English Catholics, who fancied the idea of young Mary becoming their queen. But on the other side were the English Protestant Reformers. These

Protestants were not keen on a Catholic with Mary's credentials (queen of one of England's oldest enemies and joint heir to the throne of another) becoming their new boss.

Although the English Protestant team had fewer people in it, they were stronger. The Protestants won the contest, so Mary's chances were scuppered (for now).

The Protestants got their prize of a Protestant monarch. Her name was Queen Elizabeth I, a half-sister of the late Mary Tudor . . . and a cousin of our heroine Mary. And who said royals were inbred?

The news that a Protestant had become ruler of England was greeted with cheers from Protestant Reformers across the border in Scotland.

The Scottish Protestants believed that Elizabeth could help them get rid of the Catholic religion in Scotland, too.

All of this showed that Elizabeth was a threat to Mary's future. Except nobody realised yet just how big a threat Elizabeth really was . . .

8

Ups and downs

Apart from her religion, it's hard to see at first glance what Mary had to fear from her cousin. Take the question of who was more beautiful, which was important in those days. Elizabeth had long, red-gold hair; but Mary's was an equally splendid auburn colour. And Elizabeth was shorter than Mary, which made Mary look more queenly.

To top it all, Elizabeth's complexion wasn't half as good as Mary's (and in those days people obsessed over how good a girl's complexion was).

So much for looks, but what about brains? Elizabeth was a good scholar, but Mary was bright, too.

And compared with Elizabeth, Mary's claim to the English throne was just as strong – if not stronger.

In fact, Elizabeth's ancestry was a bit of a mess. Her dad, Henry VIII, had divorced his first wife so he could marry Elizabeth's mum. It was unheard of for a king to divorce his queen in those days. So lots of people, especially Catholics, believed the marriage between Elizabeth's mum and dad had been illegal.

That meant Elizabeth, in many people's eyes, was illegitimate – not a proper heir to the throne. As if that wasn't bad enough, Henry had got bored with his new marriage and ordered Elizabeth's mum's head to be chopped off! Not exactly a thumbs-up to his daughter.

But now Elizabeth had her bum on the throne she was determined to stay there. Luckily for her, she had a crafty adviser to whisper schemes in her ear about how to keep Mary at bay. His name was William Cecil, Elizabeth's chief minister.

Throughout Elizabeth's reign, Cecil tried to persuade Elizabeth to marry and give birth to an heir so Mary's claim would disappear. But given that Elizabeth's very own dad had been a nutter who had executed her mother in cold blood, persuading Elizabeth to trust any man as her husband was easier said than done!

Meanwhile, back in France, Mary got caught up in a whirlwind of dramatic events. They began on 10 July 1559, when King Henri croaked after being injured a few days earlier in a jousting competition.

His death meant the dauphin became King François of France . . . and the sixteen-year-old Mary at last became a double queen.

Now that Mary was queen of Scots and queen of France, her Catholic supporters called for Elizabeth to step aside and make way for Mary to become queen of England, too. Suddenly, it seemed as though Mary's star was on the rise.

Well, not quite. Mary's title of queen of France didn't give her much real power. The person who really ruled France was François' nasty and scheming mother, Catherine de Medici, who felt threatened by Mary and didn't like her at all.

Then there was more bad news, this time from Scotland. On 11 June 1560 somebody who loved Mary very deeply died – her mother, Mary of Guise.

But there was worse to come. In mid November, François, who had always been sickly, returned home from a hunting expedition complaining of dizziness and a buzzing noise in his ear.

A few days later, he collapsed in church with an intense headache. The poor soul probably had an abscess in his brain. He died in his bed a month short of his seventeenth birthday on Thursday, 5 December 1560.

Mary was suddenly a widow and no longer queen of France. Catherine de Medici became regent and told Mary to sling her hook. Mary was forced to hand back all the French crown jewels.

Mary wasn't welcome at the French royal court and she certainly wasn't welcome in England. So where would she go now?

9

As soon as news spread that the hot young queen of Scots was a free agent, marriage offers began flooding in from all over Europe.

Quick off the mark was the king of Denmark, whose seafaring country promised Mary a life of shellfish, sausages and beer.

Not to be outdone, the Danish king's next-door neighbour, the king of Sweden, got in on the act. Life in his land of forests and lakes offered up such treasures as pickled herring, spicy vodka and, no doubt, very smart furniture – an old-fashioned version of the Swedish stuff you can buy in Ikea, perhaps?

Then there was the duke of Ferrara, a beautiful Italian city, who wooed Mary with the promise of huge banquets and fine wines.

More beer and sausages were on offer from the duke of Bavaria in Germany, while Ferdinand I, the Holy Roman Emperor (a *seriously* big fish), also tried his luck.

So which one got lucky?

Incredibly, none of them. Mary just didn't believe any of these chaps was right for her. Instead, she had her heart set on the familiar taste of Highland venison in the land of mountains, moors and mists. In other words, Mary wanted to return home to Scotland.

When Mary's French relatives found out she had turned down almost every eligible royal bachelor in Europe, they begged her to change her mind. Her Guise uncles tried to persuade her to forget about dreich and drizzly Scotland and choose a life in the sun, by marrying into the powerful Spanish royal family.

But Mary believed her uncles were just interested in what was good for them. So she stuck to her guns and sailed for home.

10

A noisy homecoming

It was damp and grey on Tuesday, 19 August 1561, when Mary's boat arrived at Edinburgh's port of Leith. It was thirteen years since Mary had last seen her homeland. She had left as a girl, now she returned as a woman. At last, it was time to begin her rule as Mary, Queen of Scots.

If Mary was expecting a welcoming party, she was disappointed. Not a soul turned out to greet her as she stepped onto the wet cobbles. Why? Because Mary's boat had arrived a week ahead of schedule, so the Scots simply weren't ready for her.

Not to be put off, the queen and her companions borrowed some horses and rode up to the Palace of Holyroodhouse in Edinburgh. By the evening, rumours spread that the queen had come home and people began to celebrate with bonfires and music.

But not everybody was pleased. Yes, you guessed it, the Reformers were up in arms that the Catholic queen had returned. A mob of grumpy Reformers even gathered outside her window at night, determined to make sure she couldn't get a good sleep.

They played fiddles and other instruments while singing

psalms so badly out of tune that even the local cat population must have protested. One person who heard the noise wrote that 'nothing could be worse'.

Despite the racket, Mary must have felt quite at home in Holyrood. The palace was designed to look French, so she got used to it quickly – especially since she had also brought several servants and friends over with her from France.

The French atmosphere in Mary's royal court also annoyed the Reformers – it showed Mary was determined to stick with the Catholic religion.

But Mary refused to be cowed by the mob. Instead, she concentrated on those who wished her well, which was actually most people. To make up for the lack of fanfare when Mary arrived, the bigwigs in Edinburgh organised a street party for her.

And what a party it was. There was enough food and wine to feed an army, there were loads of people in fancy dress and there was endless music and dancing. Fifty townsmen wore costumes to make them look like Moors, a mysterious and exotic people from the Mediterranean. Mary loved fancy dress, and, making her official entrance into the city, she led these weird and wonderful jokers up Edinburgh's Royal Mile.

There was laughter everywhere, except for the moment when some glum children were ordered by the Reformers to give the queen a Protestant Bible to try to change her mind about her religion. The kids were also commanded to chant nasty things about Mary's Catholic beliefs.

It was a cheap trick and it didn't work. Just as the Reformers showed they were determined to keep bugging Mary until she changed her religion, so she made it clear they were wasting their time. Once a headstrong teenager, the queen was now a stubborn young woman.

Mary had good reason to be angry. She didn't want to change anybody else's religion, so why should she have to change hers? What business was it of anybody else if Catholic mass was said in Mary's own private household?

Except Mary's wasn't just any household. Who else could afford to decorate their homes with more than a hundred tapestries, or have space for forty-five beds with gold and silver lace trimmings? Where else could you find a woman who was carried about on a horse-drawn litter covered with velvet and fringed with gold and silk? Who else in Scotland had a coach that looked like a four-poster bed on wheels?

Nobody else had all these things, of course, because they were luxuries fit only for a queen. And being queen meant Mary was expected to set an example to the rest of the kingdom. So because her religion was considered old hat or just plain wrong by certain powerful people, Mary had a real problem on her hands.

Luckily, Mary had a special place where she could take her mind off such troubles. It was called a wardrobe . . .

11

Masks and disguises

Like most young women, Mary loved clothes. Unlike most young women, Mary had a giant wardrobe. It was so huge, you could get lost in it. There were dozens of gowns, petticoats, chemises (under-dresses), silk stockings, silk garters and Spanish farthingales (sets of wooden hoops made to support wide underskirts).

Then there were thirty-six pairs of velvet shoes laced with silver and gold, to be worn with dresses made from cloth of silver or gold, silk, satin, velvet or damask (a fancy, expensive woven cloth). To cap it all, Mary had dozens of hats, umpteen pairs of perfumed gloves, riding clothes – you name it . . . she wore it.

Actually, Mary had more clothes than she could ever wear, while a typical poor woman in an Edinburgh close or wynd just up the road might own only one dress, which she had to make herself.

Mary's lifestyle was a million miles away from some of the subjects living on her doorstep, yet Mary was keen to see what life was like for poorer people. One of the most exciting ways of doing this was to wear a disguise.

Along with the four Marys, the queen once went to Stirling dressed up as a beggar to see who would give her money. Mary and her pals also pretended to be the wives of important Edinburgh townsmen and got up to all sorts of mischief.

Mary even disguised herself as a man so she could walk about Edinburgh and see things from a man's point of view.

Mary was such a master of disguise that some people began to wonder who the real Mary was. The queen loved pretending to be somebody she wasn't and expected others to do the same. So she held lots of masked balls, called masques, and invited all the important nobles of the day to attend.

Some of those who turned up had a lot to hide under their masks. They pretended to be friendly to Mary, but underneath they had bad intentions.

Take Lord James Stuart, for example. This was Mary's older half-brother, who had a claim to her throne. Behind his mask of politeness, Lord James was a scheming rat who wanted rid of Mary so he could become monarch himself.

Men like Lord James

might have been dastardly swine, but at least they treated Mary with some courtesy (for now, anyway).

But there was one man who entered Mary's life who was no fan of masked balls or any kind of partying. He did nothing to disguise the fact that he hated everything about Mary and became hell-bent on destroying her. His name was John Knox.

12

Nasty Knox

Dressed in black robes and black hat, with a long bristly beard that shoogled when he ranted (which was often), John Knox seemed like the nastiest man in Scotland. In fact, there was a good side to Knox, which came up with some bright ideas. But, whenever he dealt with Mary, he kept his good side well hidden under a cloak of villainy.

Knox was the Protestant minister of St Giles Cathedral, just up the road from Holyroodhouse. He spent a lot of his time preaching to the crowds in his cathedral about why Mary should be got rid of. People began listening to what he had to say, which made him very dangerous.

Mary reminded Knox of the three things he hated most in life, and Knox used these things to attack her in his sermons:

1. The French – Knox said Mary's French courtiers were a bad influence on Scotland. So what was Knox's beef with France? Was it because he didn't like snails or frogs' legs? Was it because he thought French people shrug too often?

The other reason Knox hated France was because it was still under the shadow of . . .

2. The Catholic Church.

In fact, Knox feared the mass like black magic. And he hated the leader of the Catholic Church – the pope. (To think Knox had once been a Catholic priest himself!)

Knox encouraged people to smash up Catholic churches and throw their statues and decorations away. Knox's supporters called this iconoclasm, but to Mary it was nothing but vandalism.

One of the things Knox especially despised about the Catholic Church was the honourable place it gave to . . .

3. Women – Knox said women were weak, stupid and had no right to rule a kingdom. Today, he would be regarded as a male chauvinist pig. Or just a nutter.

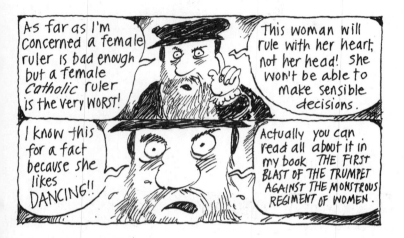

Imagine the scene when Mary finally came face to face with nasty Knox. Did Mary end up a quivering wreck while the rampant Reformer tore strips off her? Was she cowed into changing her religion and flinging her French courtiers out onto the street? Not a bit of it.

The fiery preacher was met by an ice-cool queen, as Mary gave as good as she got. She held her ground as they argued about religion, the French and whether men were better than women.

Mary proved men were no better than women by making sure Knox never won an argument between them! In fact, Mary always wanted to get the last word, even if it meant bringing her enemies back from the dead so they could hear it . . .

13

The corpse on trial

Mary soon discovered she had enemies all over the country. She became determined to punish them – and even chased some beyond the grave.

One such case began when Mary travelled north to the Highlands to see the rest of her kingdom. In those days, most of Scotland's population lived up north. People there quite liked the French and were almost all still Catholics.

So Mary had nothing to fear, right? Wrong. Sure, in many places Mary was welcomed, but not everywhere. Some Highland Catholic nobles were unhappy with her.

One in particular, the earl of Huntly, was very angry – mainly because the queen had taken some of his land away.

She had given it to her half-brother Lord James and made him earl of Moray to try to keep him happy, so he wouldn't plot against her. The result was one seriously huffy Huntly.

When the Queen turns up at Inverness tell the Constable at the castle not to let her in!

Yes, Lord Huntly.

But Mary returned the next day with an army to break into the castle. For obeying his master, the hapless constable was hanged by Mary's men (who were egged on by scheming Moray).

Huntly now realised he was in a tight spot. He decided attack was the best form of defence – and hatched a plot to kidnap the queen! But Mary discovered the conspiracy and ordered an army to hunt Huntly down.

Huntly was eventually caught – but the stress was too much for him and he promptly died from a stroke while sitting on his horse. But that wasn't the end of the matter. The authorities had strange ideas about crime and punishment in the sixteenth century, none of which were really Mary's fault.

Huntly's corpse was taken to Edinburgh to be put on trial. Yes, you didn't misread that last sentence – Huntly's dead body was put on trial. His coffin was kept upright so that it looked like the body inside was standing to face the charges against it.

If Huntly's ghost was listening, even it would have been spooked by the verdict – the corpse was declared 'guilty' of treason. But how do you punish a dead person? You can't, so you punish his family instead. The Huntly clan had their land taken away, while the outlaw chief was finally buried.

To take her mind off such ghoulish goings-on, Mary liked to go out horse-riding. Other outdoor pursuits that set her mind at ease included hawking, archery and golf.

When the weather wasn't good enough for outdoor sports, Mary liked playing games indoors. These games had a lot to teach Mary. For example:

1. Chess – stay a step ahead of your opponent and don't get backed into a corner.

2. Cards – you win some, you lose some, and often there's not a lot you can do about it.

3. Billiards – one slip-up could lose you the match, so you need to keep your head . . .

So was Mary any good at these games? The rest of this story contains a few clues. But first she was ready to open a new chapter in her life. Her husband François had long since died, but she was still a young woman who craved romance and security – especially since there were so many creeps around trying to give her a hard time.

The fact is, Mary needed a new husband. But who would want to marry her?

14

Hunt for a husband

Mary was a widow, but she was still younger and more beautiful than many first-time brides. She was, after all, only twenty. And, let's not forget, she was a queen. That made her very fanciable!

But it wasn't just her Scottish kingdom that made Mary good wife material. She knew her claim to the English throne went down well with suitors – probably more so, since England was larger and wealthier than Scotland.

To try to give her image a boost, Mary wrote to Elizabeth asking her to name Mary as the official heir to the English throne:

Dear Cousin Elizabeth,
Since you have no kids, perhaps you could name me as next in line to the throne of England? It would go down so well with a future husband.
yours Cousin Mary

> Dear Cousin Mary,
> Let's talk. But not now, I'm busy.
> yours Cousin Elizabeth

Mary had to keep asking Elizabeth when they were going to talk about her request, but Elizabeth just kept putting it off. The reason Elizabeth got cold feet wasn't so much that she didn't think Mary was a worthy heir, it was that she didn't want *anyone* to be her heir.

Elizabeth was very superstitious. She feared naming her heir would tempt fate, and she would die as a result. That's why Elizabeth never wanted to get married and have children. She believed someone would try to get rid of her as soon as she gave birth and put her child on the throne instead.

In a way, Elizabeth and Mary were in the same boat. They were both expected to have a husband because, as we have discovered, people believed queens were not strong enough to rule on their own without a king. The difference was Mary really wanted to tie the knot.

The question was, who would she marry? And what religion would he be? Catholics wanted her to marry a Catholic (what a surprise), but who did Protestants want her to marry? Was it:

A.   A Scientologist.

B.   A Protestant.

C.   A vegetarian.

Given that A hadn't been invented yet and C isn't actually a religion, you guessed correctly. One Protestant who wasn't shy of voicing his opinion on this matter was Mr Knox. And guess what – Mary and Knox had another argument.

Knox wasn't the only nutter who stuck his oar into Mary's marriage plans. Now that Mary was a free agent, she began attracting some pretty loopy admirers.

Take the poet Pierre de Chastelard, for example. Like a lovesick puppy, de Chastelard was found hiding under Mary's bed. Unlike a puppy, he was armed with a knife. De Chastelard was given a rap across the knuckles but allowed to go free since he'd caused no real harm.

But Mary's advisers clearly didn't understand that they had a stalker on their hands. Two days later, while Mary was staying in Fife, de Chastelard crept into her bedroom again . . . just as the queen was getting undressed. Oops!

Grabbed by the royal bodyguards, the hapless poet was dragged off and tried for treason.

Even after de Chastelard was taken away to be executed, Mary was left too frightened to sleep on her own. So she had Mary Fleming, one of the four Marys, sleep beside her in her room for months.

The queen got no sympathy, though, from nasty Knox. He said it was her own fault she attracted weirdos and creeps. Looking at Knox, Mary probably agreed he had a point.

Another busybody who interfered in Mary's marriage plans was Elizabeth.

The cheek of it! She refused to help her cousin out, but still stuck her nose into Mary's affairs.

Elizabeth's worry was simple – Mary might marry a powerful European prince or king. If that happened, it would make Scotland stronger and England would be under threat.

So Elizabeth wrote Mary letters which went a bit like this:

Dear Cousin Mary,
I hear you are on the lookout for a new husband.
Well, before you get any ideas, let's get one thing straight:
I'm bigger than you (okay, I hear you're taller but I mean
I'm more powerful) and I'm not going to let you marry
someone whose kingdom is a threat to England.
That means you can forget about getting hitched to any
royals from France, Spain or Austria. Got it?

I have selected a suitable husband for you. He's an
English Protestant called Lord Robert Dudley. Now, if you
marry him, I might just recognize you as my heir.

But if you don't marry someone suitable, I will
INVADE Scotland!!

Glad I could help you reach a sensible decision,
love Cousin Elizabeth

And you thought your relatives were strange! This was a gross insult to Mary. Especially since Elizabeth had a sneaky reason for wanting Dudley to become Mary's husband – Dudley and Elizabeth were lovers, and Elizabeth wanted to use Dudley to bring Scotland more under her control.

But Mary wasn't born yesterday, and she angrily wrote back to Elizabeth.

Mary's replies went something like this:

Dear Cousin Elizabeth,
You've got a nerve telling me what to do! Especially
as we've never even met! I don't want to marry Dudley
and he doesn't want to marry me. Got it ?!!

Now, if you really insist I marry an Englishman,
there is one English bloke I fancy – his name is Darnley...

15

Dashing Darnley

Henry Stuart, Lord Darnley, was drop-dead gorgeous. Mary first clapped eyes on him in February 1565, at a village in Fife, while she was out on a winter hunt. It wasn't long before they broke the ice and got chatting.

Mind you, not everyone thought Darnley was a hunk. Sir James Melville, one of Mary's gossiping courtiers, certainly didn't think he was that great.

Ah, Sir James Melville, do tell us about this Darnley fellow!

The Queen thinks he's the lustiest and best-proportioned, lang (tall) man she has seen.

Personally, I think he's more like a woman than a man—beardless and baby-faced.

In those days, a lot of people thought it was very unmanly not to have a beard. But to be fair, Darnley was just seventeen.

Darnley was born and brought up in England, but he had English and Scottish royal blood. In fact, he was another of Mary's cousins. That seems a bit weird, but it was not all that unusual to go out with your cousin in Mary's day.

Anyway, Darnley's joint royal blood meant he had a claim to the English throne. While that was something else that made him attractive to Mary, Elizabeth didn't approve. So when it looked like Mary was going to go ahead and marry Darnley, Elizabeth poked her nose in again.

Elizabeth demanded that no wedding plans should be made until Elizabeth got married herself. Both Elizabeth and Mary knew that was never going to happen, so this made Mary very cross. She was fed up of Elizabeth's interference.

Mary decided to start going out with Darnley anyway. She fancied him rotten and Darnley seemed to fancy her, too. But most of all, Mary desperately wanted to get one over on that bossyboots Elizabeth.

Mary's headstrong side probably got the better of her. She was so keen to show Elizabeth that nobody could tell her what to do that she rushed into things with Darnley – and quickly decided to marry him.

But even before the wedding, Darnley started to show a dark side. Sure, he was charming enough to make sure Mary would marry him. But Darnley wasn't really in love with Mary – he was in love with himself and only wanted to marry Mary to make himself more powerful.

Once Darnley knew he was definitely going to become Mary's husband, he began to show his true colours. He drank too much wine and was very rude to Mary's friends.

Mary began to realise she didn't love Darnley, either. But there was no turning back now. At least he had nice legs.

The marriage of Mary and Darnley went ahead as planned. It was a Catholic ceremony, but Darnley showed a cunning streak by refusing to join in the Catholic mass afterwards. He wanted to avoid upsetting the powerful Protestant nobles. Darnley was neither a Protestant nor a Catholic, he just liked to lean towards whichever side had the upper hand.

The wedding was a big do, but everybody noticed that three people weren't there:

1. Elizabeth – she was still in a huff about the whole thing.

2. Knox.

3. Moray (aka Lord James), Mary's half-brother – the wedding made his own claim to the Scottish throne even weaker. In fact, Moray even started a rebellion against Mary, but it was stopped before it really got going.

The wedding ceremony was barely over before Darnley started causing trouble for Mary. He was often drunk and had a string of romantic affairs with other people.

But there was worse – Darnley tried to boss Mary about. So Mary denied him the crown matrimonial, which meant he could never be a proper king.

I want to be KING!

I want to be KING!

So was there anything good to say about this marriage? Well, at least it gave Mary an heir, when she became pregnant. Producing heirs was what royal marriages were all about, after all. Love often didn't come into it.

Now that Mary was due to have a child of her own, it made her stronger – especially where the throne of England was concerned. She began making comments that she was the rightful queen of England and played up her Catholic religion to get other Catholic kingdoms on her side.

But Mary soon found that trying to turn the religious tide back in favour of the Catholic Church had deadly consequences.

16

Murder at court

Mary gave Catholics important jobs at her royal court to impress other Catholic kingdoms and show the Protestant Reformers that, frankly, she was fed up with them. The trouble was, some Protestant nobles were determined to stop at *nothing* to get rid of Catholicism . . . even murder.

These Protestant lords blamed one man for encouraging Mary to make her court more Catholic. He was an Italian called David Rizzio. Rizzio was Mary's private secretary and one of her closest friends. His surname was pronounced 'Rit-see-oh'.

To try to get rid of Rizzio, Mary's Protestant enemies made up all sorts of stories about him, like Mary and Rizzio were secretly boyfriend and girlfriend. That was a lie, but if it was meant to make drunken Darnley furious with jealousy, it worked. Before long, Rizzio had a long list of enemies out to get him – especially Darnley.

Things came to a head on 9 March 1566. It was a Saturday evening, and Mary and Rizzio were sitting down to dinner with some other friends in Mary's privy (private) chamber. Mary's big belly showed her baby was due any day now.

Suddenly, Darnley appeared, and went up to speak to Mary. Then, while Darnley distracted the queen, a group of Protestant nobles sneaked in and began pushing Rizzio around.

A furious argument started and Rizzio hid behind his queen's back, as she protected her terrified friend.

But the group of nobles lunged at Rizzio and began stabbing him with daggers until he fell to the floor, dead. As the cold iron blades flashed in front of her, Mary was terrified and thought she would be killed, too.

The thugs didn't want to kill Mary, though – just scare her so she would change her Catholic ways. Besides, there was no way Darnley would have let any harm come to his unborn baby, because being the father of Mary's heir would help Darnley become a proper king. And the Protestant lords didn't want any harm to come to the baby, either, because they planned to make him into a Protestant king one day.

Not that any of that had helped poor Rizzio – who was stabbed fifty-six times! So had Darnley actually done any of the stabbing? Apparently not, but he was still guilty of helping the Protestant nobles commit murder.

Darnley tried to worm his way out of the crime by telling Mary he had thought the nobles would just rough Rizzio up a bit – not *murder* him. Unfortunately, however, somebody sent Mary a very interesting item in the post:

Mary's blood ran cold, but she knew she didn't have the strength to punish Darnley right now. She had a baby to give birth to. So, for now, a truce was agreed.

17

Mother Mary

Giving birth in the sixteenth century involved three things – agonising pain, lots of blood-curdling screams and a high risk neither mum nor baby would survive.

Luckily, after a long and painful labour, Mary successfully gave birth to a son on Wednesday, 19 June 1566. He was named James, the new heir to the throne.

On the streets of Edinburgh, people celebrated by lighting bonfires. But when the news reached Elizabeth in England she gave it a frosty reception. Elizabeth knew the baby made Mary stronger, and left Elizabeth looking weak in comparison.

Right away, Mary handed baby James over to two friends, the earl of Mar and his wife, for safekeeping. It was normal for a queen not to look after her own baby, but it was even more important now that Mary's life was becoming more dangerous.

As soon as James was born, Mary and Darnley's truce was over. Whenever they were in the same room, they just argued. So from now on, they spent as little time together as possible.

Mary became worried that Darnley might kidnap James,

especially now that Darnley was closer to her Protestant enemies than ever. So Mary made sure James was taken to the security of Stirling Castle.

Once Mary felt her baby was safe, she tried to relax a bit by hunting in Perthshire. But it wasn't easy to relax when her horrible husband kept stressing her out!

Darnley was determined to become a proper king and threatened to separate from Mary, which would disgrace her. Meanwhile, Mary tried to get on with being a good queen by visiting local courts in the Borders, but it was impossible to take her mind off her troubles at home and her stress levels got higher.

One day, Mary collapsed, vomited blood and then passed out. When she woke up, she couldn't see or speak. She felt certain she was going to die.

Fortunately, Mary had a brilliant French doctor called Charles Nau, who worked out what was wrong with her and set about making her better. Mary probably had a stomach ulcer that had burst because her body was so stressed out about her marriage. The bleeding had given her body a toxic shock. Very nasty.

Mary had narrowly escaped death and was lucky to be alive, yet she was very depressed. She felt trapped by her marriage, as Darnley's behaviour got worse. He was such a nasty piece of work, even the Protestant lords were now fed up with him.

A lot of people began wishing Darnley would just disappear. After all, now that he had given Mary a son and heir, he wasn't really needed any more . . .

18

Out with a bang

Darnley had no idea how much trouble he was in, and carried on behaving like an oaf. Mary would have divorced him if she could, but divorce would have gone down like a lead balloon with her Catholic supporters.

Instead, she could have got something called an annulment, which was a way of ending her marriage without upsetting the Catholic Church too much. But an annulment had a problem – it would make baby James illegitimate, and therefore not a proper heir to the throne. That was the last thing Mary wanted.

So, Mary was stuck with Darnley – unless somebody could come up with another way to get rid of him.

In the meantime, baby James was baptised a Catholic in a lavish ceremony. Everybody noticed two people didn't turn up – Elizabeth, who really ought to have been there since she was the godmother, and Darnley, which was a poor show given that he was . . . the father.

But Elizabeth was *still* in the huff, while Darnley had, by now, lost the plot. Enraged with Mary, he was banging on more than ever about wanting to become a proper king.

Mary became even more worried that Darnley might

kidnap James, so she made sure her husband was kept where she could keep an eye on him. This was made easier by the fact Darnley was now suffering from a serious disease called syphilis, which gave him smelly, puss-filled pimples all over his body. He was so vain, he was actually happy that Mary wanted him kept behind closed doors, away from the royal court.

The couple went to stay in a place called Kirk o' Field House, in Edinburgh. (Though they were barely speaking to each other, they still lived at the same address.) Mary slept in a room beneath her husband's.

Eventually, Darnley began to get better, and on 9 February 1567 he celebrated that he would soon be able to return to normal life (or as normal as Darnley's life could ever be) at Holyroodhouse. What he didn't know was that he was about to be killed the very next day.

In the early hours of 10 February, Mary was away at a masked-ball wedding reception. Meanwhile, Darnley and his servants were left at Kirk o' Field alone.

Suddenly, at just after two o'clock in the morning, there was a huge explosion. The house at Kirk o' Field was reduced to a pile of smoke and rubble. Darnley was killed, but exactly how he died remains a mystery – a case for a historical detective.

If you want to try to solve this case, you are faced with two possible scenarios:

1 DID THE EXPLOSION KILL DARNLEY?

THERE'S NO DOUBT IT WAS A DELIBERATE EXPLOSION – BARRELS OF GUNPOWDER HAD BEEN PLACED IN THE CELLAR OF THE HOUSE.

HOWEVER, THE BODIES OF DARNLEY AND ONE OF HIS SERVANTS WERE FOUND OUTSIDE – ABOUT 40 FEET (10 METRES) AWAY.

THEY COULD HAVE BEEN THROWN THERE BY THE EXPLOSION... BLAM!

... BUT, THERE WERE NO BURNS OR BRUISES ON THE BODIES. THAT LEADS US TO...

2 DID DARNLEY AND HIS MAN ESCAPE BEFORE THE EXPLOSION ONLY TO BE KILLED BY OTHER MEANS?

DARNLEY'S CORPSE WAS FOUND, STILL DRESSED IN HIS NIGHT-SHIRT, BESIDE A TREE.

NEXT TO HIM WERE THE FOLLOWING ITEMS:
CHAIR ROPE DAGGER

THERE WERE NO STAB WOUNDS ON DARNLEY'S BODY, THOUGH.. Hmm...

It's clear from both possible scenarios that Darnley was definitely murdered. But which one is correct?

Well, think about the second scenario. Imagine Darnley had heard his assassins coming to set off the gunpowder. He and the servant then tried to escape, bringing a dagger for protection, and got out of the house before the bomb went off. But the attackers caught up with them and strangled them using the rope, tied to the tree, with the chair as a scaffold.

If that sounds far-fetched, here's another clue – why would Darnley's body end up still in one piece, and without any burns, if it was blown up in an explosion big enough to destroy a house? Surely he would have lost a leg, at least? It does seem more likely that Darnley was strangled, especially since some reports claim that his body was found with marks on his neck.

Whichever way it happened, Mary's royal court was becoming a pretty dangerous place to be. That was the second murder in less than a year!

The next question in the Darnley murder investigation is, whodunit? This is a tricky one.

Perhaps Elizabeth ordered the murder to get Mary into trouble? It turns out Elizabeth's close adviser, Cecil, knew Darnley was going to be killed before it happened. He had known Rizzio would be killed, too.

Yet Cecil didn't lift a finger to warn Mary. He much preferred to let the killings go ahead so that Mary would end up quarrelling with her nobles over who was to blame, leaving her with no time to chase after Elizabeth's crown. Given that we know Cecil was aware of what was going on, who's to say Elizabeth wasn't behind it all?

The other key suspect is Mary. But she denied this. Mary seemed to believe Darnley's assassins had actually been after her, and it was only by being away at the wedding party that she survived. She believed she had cheated death again (having done it before when she was ill) and that God had spared her life.

What's more, Mary ordered a full investigation (even though many of the investigators were really suspects themselves!) and she also offered a reward to anybody who came forward with clues.

But was Mary really as innocent as she made out? Let's face it, she *hated* Darnley and must have prayed for him to die a thousand times. Mary certainly behaved very suspiciously after the murder was over, and that soon set tongues wagging.

It was five days before Mary even ordered black taffeta to cover her walls and windows, which a Scottish queen in mourning was *expected* to put on display. And Darnley wasn't even given a state funeral, which meant he was buried quietly without any of the pomp that would *normally* accompany the funeral of a queen's husband.

To cap it all, Mary gave away some of Darnley's clothes and horses to a man called James Hepburn, the fourth earl of Bothwell. This was suspicious because Bothwell was also a suspect in the case. Darnley's tailor announced with a sniff that the clothes of the dead man had been given to the executioner.

The tailor had a point. If there was a prime suspect for Darnley's murder, then Bothwell was it.

The murder of Darnley had probably been organised before Christmas at Craigmillar Castle, near Edinburgh. A group of nobles including Bothwell were staying there at the time.

The plot was known as the Craigmillar Bond. It was cooked up right under the nose of Mary, who was also staying at the castle for a while. Did she get a whiff of what Bothwell and the others were up to?

19

Bothwell the brainy brute

Bothwell, many people believed, had Darnley's blood on his hands. He was Mary's most loyal privy counsellor – in other words, her closest adviser. He was a strong, violent man with dark hair and a bristling moustache. He was always getting into fights . . . and he hated Darnley's guts.

But if Bothwell was guilty, that pointed the finger back at Mary. Rumours were flying around that Bothwell and Mary had become boyfriend and girlfriend. If Bothwell had planned to kill Darnley, people thought, he surely must have told Mary. And that would make Mary guilty of helping to murder her husband.

So how did Mary become so close to Bothwell? How could she fall for such a brute? Well, there was more to Bothwell than a bad temper. He had a good side, too.

Bothwell was handsome, intelligent and spoke French beautifully, which gave him a lot in common with Mary. Sure, he was a Protestant, but he didn't like Protestant England and wanted Scotland to stay close to France. So he was the kind of Protestant Mary could get along with.

Above all, although he was arrogant, Bothwell seemed to be a man of honour. And Mary appreciated that. While other men brought Mary nothing but grief, Bothwell, who was seven years older than Mary, was the one man she could rely on. He had cared for her when she was ill, protected her from her enemies and advised her when she was in trouble. No wonder Mary called him her 'rock'.

And Mary clung to her rock like a limpet. Once, after Bothwell had been seriously injured in a sword fight, Mary had ridden her horse sixty miles just to be by his side. How romantic.

Yet Mary was also blind to Bothwell's bad behaviour. He got himself into a lot of criminal scrapes, but Mary acted like these were just harmless pranks.

Which takes us back to our investigation – was Bothwell the murderer? The truth is Bothwell probably took part, but didn't act alone. Many other nobles were involved. Mary's scheming half-brother Moray, for example, knew about the plot but did nothing to stop it.

Of course, Moray did his best to point the finger of

blame squarely at Bothwell. This was all part of a fiendish plan by Moray to ruin Mary's reputation and get his hands on her crown.

As rumours of Bothwell's guilt grew stronger, notices began appearing all over Edinburgh. They went a bit like this:

To make matters worse, Darnley's family arranged for a man to prowl the streets of the capital every night calling for vengeance against Bothwell. In reply, Bothwell swore that if he ever met the people responsible for writing nasty notices about him, he would wash his hands in their blood!

Eventually, Bothwell was hauled up before a court. He was let off, but that only made people suspicious that Mary had got him off the hook. After his trial, the first thing Bothwell did was nail a notice of his own to the door of the Edinburgh Tollbooth, an important public building where large crowds often gathered. It went a bit like this:

The trouble for Bothwell was that hardly anyone believed he was innocent. It was now becoming really dangerous for Mary to be bosom buddies with him. If she didn't want people to suspect her of Darnley's murder she had to end her affair with Bothwell before it was too late. At least, that was the sensible advice.

But since when could anyone tell Mary what to do? Now that her life was getting really stormy, she was more determined than ever to cling to her 'rock' . . .

20

Third time lucky?

It was the biggest mistake Mary ever made. Before her official forty days of mourning for Darnley were over, she and Bothwell were seen out as a couple. It caused a huge scandal. The queen had thrown in her lot with the man many people believed had murdered her husband.

People thought Mary was reckless. But put yourself in her shoes – without Bothwell, she must have felt so alone:

Who could blame her? Bothwell seemed like Mary's knight in shining armour, always protecting her. What's more, he said no true Scot should ever try to harm their queen. Mary believed Bothwell was the only person who could save her from meeting the same grisly fate as Darnley. And that, it seems, is why Mary fell in love with him.

On the other hand, just because Mary was in love with Bothwell, it didn't mean she wanted to *marry* him. Aged just twenty-four, Mary had already been through two disastrous marriages and enough scandal to last a lifetime. Besides, Bothwell was already married. But Bothwell had other ideas.

One day, while Mary was returning to Edinburgh after visiting her baby James at Stirling, she was unexpectedly met by Bothwell. What happened next ensured that Mary would never see her baby son again.

Bothwell hurried Mary off to his own house where he begged her to marry him. Mary wanted to leave, but wasn't allowed. It was a strange kind of kidnapping – Mary was in love with Bothwell, but she was scared of him, too.

After a lot of pleading (and a few threats), Mary was eventually persuaded . . . and Bothwell became Mary's third husband. Although she had serious reservations, she thought at least this would be a way of giving birth to more royal heirs – which would make her stronger in the long run.

Needless to say, however, there were a few obstacles on the way to the altar that Mary had to sort out:

Memo

Things to do to clear a path to the altar...

obstacle No. 1   Bothwell already married.   — He's a Protestant so he can get a divorce. I've got him a Catholic annulment, just for good measure   SORTED ✓

obstacle No 2   Bothwell not high enough rank to marry a queen.   — I've made him Duke of Orkney   SORTED ✓

obstacle No.3   Bothwell needs approval from Scottish nobles.   — I don't know how he did it – but Bothwell has persuaded nobles to sign a bond supporting him!   SORTED ✓

obstacle No 4   The Dean of St Giles' Church has to announce the marriage – he's an old pal of John Knox and is dead against it.   Bothwell threatened to bump off the Dean unless he co-operated.   SORTED ✓

All problems solved !!

Well, actually, no. Their real problems were just about to begin. Hardly anybody turned up to the wedding at Holyroodhouse. As far as most people were concerned, Bothwell had forced the queen to marry him too soon after his divorce – and she had certainly married him too quickly after Darnley's murder. It was only three months ago, for goodness sake!

And while you might expect that having a Protestant wedding ceremony was a good way for Mary to win over her enemies, all it did was annoy her Catholic friends.

As if all that weren't bad enough, the marriage started falling apart almost as soon as it began. Nasty placards were still being put up saying Bothwell was a killer, but now they included Mary, too.

Under the pressure, Bothwell's dark side began to take over. Even though Mary was his wife, Bothwell had not been given the title of king – and that made him very jealous. He wanted to act like a king, but felt inferior.

The couple had raging arguments. Mary, if she wasn't involved in Darnley's murder, might have begun to realise that jealous Bothwell probably had more to do with it than he let on. Their angry rows made Mary so upset she threatened to kill herself!

Then Mary's lifelong friends, fed up with Bothwell acting like he ruled the place, began deserting her. Even one of the four Marys, Mary Fleming, her dear old pal and cousin, decided enough was enough and left the queen's side.

Mary's stormy life was destroying everything around her. It was now only a matter of time before her whole kingdom was torn apart.

21

Civil war

Mary's disastrous third marriage had serious consequences. Some powerful Protestant nobles called the Confederate Lords got together and decided drastic action was needed to put the monarchy on the right track.

They believed Bothwell was too big for his boots, and decided that Mary was a weak and unsuitable queen – she had made too many bad decisions and still showed no sign of giving up her Catholic faith.

The Confederate Lords came up with a battle plan to get rid of Bothwell and replace Mary with her baby son, who would be turned into a Protestant and then crowned as king. They started putting their plan into action by setting up a rival royal court in the name of Prince James and recruiting an army.

While the Confederates sharpened their swords, Mary and Bothwell realised they weren't safe in Edinburgh any more. So they left for a hideout called Borthwick Castle, twelve miles south of the capital.

Built in 1430, Borthwick had walls that were tall and strong – and its gate was protected by a drawbridge.

But it wasn't long before the Confederates turned up and laid siege to the castle.

Since you can only survive in a castle for so long without fresh supplies, Mary was eventually forced to escape. Once again, she became a master of disguise and slipped out dressed as a man, without anyone noticing her.

Mary was now an outlaw in her own kingdom. To get back in control, she needed an army of her own. Luckily, there were still many people about who supported her and didn't like the Confederates. With Bothwell's help, an army of Mary's supporters was recruited. To show that this army was on Mary's side, historians later decided to give them a name that was easy to remember. Something that sounded like Mary, say . . .

A. The Marians.

B. The Martians.

C. The Marigolds.

Marians seemed like a sensible choice, and the Marian army duly went to meet the Confederates in battle. Scotland was now a kingdom at war.

It was a hot June day in 1567 when the Marians and the Confederates, who were known at the time as 'the Queen's men' and 'the King's men', met at Carberry Hill near Musselburgh.

The stage was set for a great battle. Or was it? The trouble was, nobody wanted to make the first move. Instead, the two armies just stood around, glowering at each other.

Eventually, it was suggested that Bothwell should settle things by having a duel with one of the Confederate Lords. But Mary wouldn't let him. If Bothwell was killed, she thought, then she would be in an even tighter spot.

So Mary came up with a plan. She offered to surrender herself to the Confederates, provided Bothwell was allowed to go free. This was agreed.

Mary hoped Bothwell would get the Marian army back together again later to crush the Confederates once and for all. But before Bothwell could round up Mary's soldiers for a new attack, the Confederates chased him out of the country. Mary never saw him again.

'Burn the murderess!' shouted the Confederate soldiers meanwhile as the queen was taken prisoner. They accused Mary of killing Darnley, leaving her shocked and angry.

The Confederate Lords didn't burn Mary, but instead imprisoned her in an island fortress called Loch Leven Castle. The island was tiny and the waters of Loch Leven which surrounded it were very deep. So there was not much chance of escape.

Meanwhile, Bothwell went into exile and eventually ended up across the North Sea in Denmark. Although the king of Denmark treated him well at first, Bothwell soon became a nuisance and was sent to a remote castle called Dragsholm. According to reports, he was chained to the wall of the castle dungeon until he went mad and died.

Bothwell was buried in Dragsholm church, but many centuries later his coffin was opened and his skull used as a football by local children! Bothwell's spirit was clearly not happy about this, since his ghost is said to haunt Dragsholm Castle (which is now a hotel) to this day.

22

I'm the Queen, get me out of here

Mary had plenty of time to try to guess what had happened to Bothwell as she sat in her island prison. It took her mind off the poorly furnished room she was in (no big wardrobe with lavish clothes) and the fact she had to share the castle with some of the evil Moray's family and friends.

At least Mary still had her looks (she was only twenty-four). That meant she could charm the pants of any handsome young man who came within range. One such man was George 'Pretty Geordie' Douglas, who fell for her even though he was actually part of the dreaded Moray clan. Maybe, Mary thought to herself, Pretty Geordie could be persuaded to help me escape?

While Mary was trying to get out of jail, the Confederate Lords got busy ruining her reputation and draining away her royal powers. They went around saying she was Darnley's killer (even though some of them were probably guilty themselves). They also sold off Mary's crown jewels, which were symbols of her queenly status.

One of the buyers was Elizabeth. Strange as it may seem, Elizabeth might have bought the jewels to make sure they were returned to Mary. Although the two cousins were rivals, Elizabeth still respected Mary as a fellow queen.

To see Mary imprisoned by her subjects made Elizabeth angry – and frightened. If people went around imprisoning the queen of Scots, somebody might get the same idea in England . . .

Elizabeth became even more worried when the Confederates deposed Mary and replaced her with her baby son. He was crowned James VI, the 'cradle king' on 29 July 1567 – and he was a Protestant. Elizabeth realised little James VI had a strong claim to her throne, too.

To look after the kingdom until James was old enough to run things himself, guess who got himself a job as regent? Moray, of course.

At first, Mary refused to agree to all this. Then her jailors threatened to cut her throat. So, guess what – she agreed.

Meanwhile, the Confederate Lords congratulated each other. The Catholic queen was gone and they had a new Protestant king – mission accomplished.

Or so they thought. As far as many people were concerned, Mary was still the true monarch. And Elizabeth was now so furious about what had happened she threatened to declare war on the new Scottish government.

Meanwhile, Mary hatched plans to escape. After one failed attempt to row across Loch Leven, she eventually persuaded Pretty Geordie to help her get out.

While he went off to fetch Mary's army, another doe-eyed Douglas boy called Willie rowed her across the loch. Disguised as her faithful friend Mary Seton, the queen escaped on 2 May 1568 – after a miserable eleven months in prison.

Once she was free, Mary could have fled Scotland for somewhere safe. Instead she wanted to fight for her kingdom. So she dashed off letters to friends asking for help.

Eleven days later, Mary had 6,000 Marians at her side. This proved that a lot of people in Scotland still supported her. In fact, Mary's army was far bigger than the Confederates, now led by the dreaded Moray.

A showdown was arranged at a place called Langside, near Glasgow. This was Mary's big moment. She could crush her enemies, win back her kingdom and live happily ever after with her bouncing baby boy. So what happened?

Well, her useless commander, the earl of Argyll, went and got himself ill – and Mary didn't know how to lead an army herself. So, without anyone to lead them properly, the Marians were chewed up by the Confederates like jelly babies.

Luckily, before she could be nabbed by Moray, Mary did a runner. She galloped south to Dumfries, near the border with England.

When Mary got to Dumfries, she dashed off a letter, the gist of which was:

> *Dear Cousin Elizabeth,*
> *Er... I'm in a spot of bother. I hope you don't mind but I was wondering if I could stay with you for a bit...*

23

Friend or foe?

Mary didn't have time to wait for Elizabeth's reply. On 16 May 1568 the runaway queen of Scots was bobbing about in a fishing boat, crossing the Solway Firth to England. Eventually, she put ashore near Carlisle.

Now Mary was in England, she sent another letter to Elizabeth asking for help to get her throne back. Elizabeth felt a lot of sympathy for her cousin. She realised what it must be like to be in Mary's shoes, and was just about to lend a hand when . . .

Cecil, Elizabeth's worm-tongued adviser, stuck his beak in.

So Mary was seized by Cecil's agents before she could leave Carlisle and imprisoned (again) in a castle. Cecil wanted Mary to be put on trial for adultery (cheating on Darnley) and for Darnley's murder. A guilty verdict could get her executed – and out of the way forever. But since Cecil didn't have any evidence against Mary, he needed to find a way of framing her.

Cecil turned to Mary's old enemy, Moray, to help stitch Mary up for Darnley's murder. The two fiends came up with a casket of letters, which Cecil claimed were written by Mary to Bothwell.

In truth, the 'Casket Letters' were a mish-mash of real bits written by Mary and fake bits written by somebody else. The fake bits were meant to make Mary seem guilty. The letters went a bit like this:

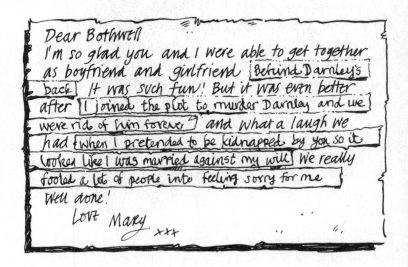

Dear Bothwell
I'm so glad you and I were able to get together as boyfriend and girlfriend [behind Darnley's back] It was such fun! But it was even better after [I joined the plot to murder Darnley and we were rid of him forever] and what a laugh we had [when I pretended to be kidnapped by you so it looked like I was married against my will] We really fooled a lot of people into feeling sorry for me
Well done!
Love Mary xxx

Cecil, Moray and the other Confederate Lords thought the Casket Letters would stitch Mary up royally. Except not even Elizabeth was convinced they were genuine. And when Mary was put on trial the letters failed to stand up in court. Mary wasn't cleared, but she wasn't found guilty, either.

Mary insisted it was Moray and the Confederates who were the real killers. She pleaded with Elizabeth to meet her so Elizabeth could hear her side of the story.

But Elizabeth was torn between sympathy and suspicion of Mary. Elizabeth refused to meet Mary, or let her out of prison. Meanwhile, Cecil persuaded Elizabeth it would be best all round if she finally accepted that the new ruler of Scotland was Moray (who ran the country on behalf of young King James).

Mary felt sad and angry. Elizabeth kept Mary prisoner but wouldn't even meet her, while she allowed a bunch of crooks to steal Mary's kingdom.

On the other hand, life in captivity was pretty cushy. Mary was allowed to carry on living like a queen and never had less than thirty servants. At her side she still had trusty friends like Mary Seton, along with Pretty Geordie and wee Willie Douglas (the lads who had helped her escape from Loch Leven Castle). Mary was even allowed out to go riding sometimes.

On the down side, Mary was always kept under guard and her letters were read. And she kept on having to move around from one small castle to another, because she had so many servants. In those days, small castles very dirty and smelly when a lot of people stayed in them for any length of time, and the drains got blocked. The only way to clean them was to get everybody out so the whole place could be fumigated.

At least there was always a feast waiting for Mary wherever she went. She had two courses at dinner, which doesn't sound like much. Except each course had sixteen different dishes in it. That's thirty-two dishes in one meal!

Since Mary wasn't allowed out riding or walking very much, she put on weight. She had a constant sore tummy and lots of aches and pains. Her long back became twisted into a slight stoop. The sicknesses she had had when she was younger returned and she became very gloomy.

As her months in captivity stretched into years, Mary became desperate to escape. She wrote letters to everyone she could think of – the Pope, the French – all begging for help. But Mary's old mother-in-law, Catherine de Medici, ignored her pleas and so did almost everyone else.

Then there was a glimmer of hope. The long war between Catholics and Protestants all over Europe began hotting up. In Spain, a very strong Catholic kingdom, the king began to talk of invading England to restore the old religion.

English Catholics began to prepare for a battle that would overthrow Elizabeth. All they needed was someone to replace her. Hmmm . . .

Luckily, Mary managed to smuggle out a few letters to the Spanish king:

Dear King of Spain,
I have been a prisoner here for many years now.
I am a hard-done-to Catholic Queen who deserves
to be set free. If only Spain would invade England,
all my troubles would be over!
Yours hopefully, Mary, Queen of Scots
P.S. If you don't invade, I'm sunk!

But Mary's luck changed when hopes of an invasion began to fade. There was nothing for her to do but take up embroidery to pass the time and look after some dogs and cats. Then, just as she was getting used to her life in prison, news crossed the channel of a dreadful event in France.

On 24 August 1572 thousands of French Protestants were sliced, skewered and splattered in a terrible killing spree by Catholics. It was called the St Bartholomew's Day Massacre.

For Mary, it couldn't have happened at a worse time.

24

The plot thickens

Panic struck Protestant England – everyone thought England's Catholic neighbours would definitely invade now. Elizabeth would be ejected and Protestants everywhere would be pulped. Suddenly, the Catholic Queen Mary became the most dangerous woman alive!

To try to make a legal case for Mary's execution, Cecil started a smear campaign against her. He published the

Casket Letters so everyone in England could read them. Even though the letters were fakes, Cecil hoped people would be fooled into thinking Mary was a murderer – and start calling for her head. But Elizabeth was having none of it.

But then more Protestants were killed in Europe. In July 1584, William of Orange, a Protestant leader in Holland, was assassinated. Again, English Protestants feared the worst and the pressure grew on Elizabeth to get rid of Mary.

Mary knew her days were numbered. So she turned to the one person she thought she could really depend on – her adult son. Now that Moray was long gone (assassinated in 1570), Mary proposed that James should share his throne with her. Except James had grown up used to the idea that he alone would rule as king.

Instead, James suggested Mary could come back to Scotland as queen mother. (This title showed she had once been queen, but was now mum to the present monarch.)

James' offer wasn't accepted. Mary thought she deserved to at least share the role of monarch, since her kingdom had been stolen from her. Now she felt that even her own son had let her down.

Mary became desperate to find another way out of prison. She was willing to listen to anybody who came up with a scheme to help her escape.

One such man was Anthony Babington, a rich young Catholic gentleman.

Unfortunately, the Babington Plot was badly organised. Not even Babington really knew what was going on and soon the whole thing fell apart.

When Cecil and his cronies, like spymaster Francis Walsingham, discovered what had been going on, they jumped with joy. Although Mary never gave her permission for the plotters to kill Elizabeth, it seems that she agreed with most of their plans. Finally, there was enough evidence against Mary to put her on trial.

Mary was accused of treason against Elizabeth and taken to court. If Mary was found guilty, the penalty was certain death.

In court, Cecil tightened his net. Mary wasn't allowed her own lawyer or witnesses. She couldn't even take notes or examine any documents. It was not a fair trial!

Mary denied plotting to kill Elizabeth, but Cecil was determined to crush her. He even made sure the English parliament asked Elizabeth to call for the executioner. Meanwhile, the Catholic powers of Europe, like Catherine de Medici, didn't lift a finger to help Mary.

Elizabeth wasn't soft on her cousin any more, but she still thought it was wrong for an anointed queen like Mary to be put to death. Elizabeth would have preferred to wait for her cousin to die of natural causes.

Eventually, Elizabeth reached a decision . . .

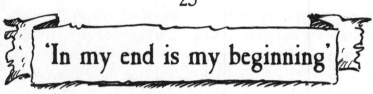

25

'In my end is my beginning'

Early in the morning of 8 February 1587, Mary was lying in her chamber in Fotheringay Castle, about seventy-five miles outside London. If she slept at all, she probably had nothing but bad dreams. But it was only when she was suddenly summoned by some of Elizabeth's men that Mary's real nightmare began.

Mary was told to get dressed and say goodbye to her servants – she wouldn't be needing them any more.

But Mary was already prepared for the day ahead. She had on stockings of sky-blue, embroidered with silver thread and held up by green silk garters. Then a bodice and a red petticoat. On top, she wore a gown made of thick black satin.

As Mary said her farewells, she noticed her servants were crying, so she told them to cheer up. But they all knew what was about to happen.

After pleading with Elizabeth's men, some of Mary's dearest companions were allowed to go with her. Mary and her friends then walked to the castle's great hall. As Mary clutched a crucifix and a Catholic prayer book, the short walk must have seemed to last forever.

In the great hall was a wooden stage, which had been specially built for the day. It was two feet (or half a metre) high and twelve feet (or four metres) square. There was a cushion for the queen to kneel on . . . and an execution block clad in black.

Around the stage was gathered a crowd of hundreds. Elizabeth was not there, though. She probably felt guilty about her decision, which was just about to be read out to everyone.

Then Mary came in. The crowd turned to look at her. Being held prisoner for nineteen years had taken its toll on Mary's looks. She was forty-four but looked much older. But at least her auburn hair seemed as beautiful as ever.

Up on the stage stood the headsman of the Tower of London and his assistant. Both men wore long black gowns with white aprons and masks over their faces, as though they were at one of Mary's fancy dress balls. Except this time nobody was pretending.

Once Mary was in position, the charge against her was

read out – she had been found guilty of treason against Queen Elizabeth and sentenced to execution by having her head chopped off. The crowd gasped, Mary started praying, and the headsman and his assistant got ready to do their dirty work.

At the last moment, one of Elizabeth's Protestant churchmen lunged towards Mary:

As Mary's gown was taken off, the crowd gasped again. People realised that the red of her petticoat was the colour of a Catholic martyr – somebody willing to die for their beliefs. It was the colour of dried blood.

Now Mary's friends were crying loudly. She comforted them and said goodbye one last time, asking them not to forget about her.

Mary knelt down and put her head on the black chopping block. The skin of her neck looked deathly white.

People craned their own necks to get a better view as the executioner raised his axe . . .

SLAM! Down came the blade upon Mary's neck. But the queen of Scots didn't die that easily – it took a second blow before her head was cut from her body.

When the executioner held up Mary's head by the hair, witnesses said her lips were still moving – as though she was still praying! People screamed in shock and horror.

Then, suddenly, the head fell out of the executioner's grasp, leaving him holding only the hair and a white cap. Mary had been wearing a wig! People screamed and gasped again, as Mary's nearly bald skull rolled onto the floor.

It was one of the most gruesome executions in history. But when Mary's head finally stopped rolling it was – at long last – finally all over.

As Mary's friends left the scene, they were devastated.

Epilogue

At last, Mary's nightmare was at an end. She was buried in Peterborough Cathedral, about seventy miles from London. Years later, in 1612, her body (head included!) was placed in a tomb in London's Westminster Abbey. There she was left to rest in peace.

But she also had some unexpected company. Elizabeth had died in 1603 and her tomb was next to her cousin's. The two great rivals were finally in the same room . . . although they didn't have much to say to each other!

Both tombs were paid for by James VI, who had inherited Scotland from his mum and England from Elizabeth (making him James I of England, too). Mary's tomb was larger and fancier than Elizabeth's. This showed that James VI, deep down, really loved his mum . . . and was rather annoyed at Elizabeth for executing her!

Mary's execution changed the world. It made people realise that kings and queens could be got rid of if they didn't like them. Before long, people started executing monarchs left, right and centre. The people began choosing their own leaders instead and, eventually, this change was called democracy – which gave everybody a say in how things were done.

So what else changed after Mary got her head chopped off? Well, the battle between Protestants and Catholics was never really won by either side. Eventually it just fizzled out, after most people decided it would be much better if everyone just tried to be nice to each other for a change.

And after a few more centuries of bickering and a handful of wars, the Scots, the English and the French all realised that neighbours really should be friends.

So, were she still around, Mary might agree that a lot of things have changed for the better since her tragic life and death. On the other hand, it's pretty hard to imagine Mary dumping her fantastic wardrobe for today's fashion of jeans and a T-shirt!